Reinventing a Forgotten Form

TILE
QUILT
Revival

Text copyright © 2010 by Carol Gilham Jones and Bobbi Finley

Artwork copyright © 2010 by C&T Publishing, Inc.

Publisher: Amy Marson

Creative Director: Gailen Runge

Acquisitions Editor: Susanne Woods

Editor: Liz Aneloski

Technical Editors: Teresa Stroin and Mary E. Flynn

Copyeditor/Proofreader: Wordfirm Inc.

Cover/Book Designer: Kristy Zacharias

Production Coordinator: Kirstie L. Pettersen

Production Editor: Alice Mace Nakanishi

Illustrator: Aliza Shalit

Photography by Christina Carty-Francis and Diane Pedersen of C&T Publishing, Inc., unless otherwise noted.

Published by C&T Publishing, Inc., P.O. Box 1456, Lafayette, CA 94549

Library of Congress Cataloging-in-Publication Data

Jones, Carol Gilham, 1946-

Tile quilt revival : reinventing a forgotten form / Carol Gilham Jones and Bobbi Finley.

    p. cm.

ISBN 978-1-57120-801-9 (soft cover)

1. Appliqué. 2. Quilting. I. Finley, Bobbi, 1936- II. Title.

TT779.J68 2010

746.44'5041--dc22

                    2009020106

Printed in China

10 9 8 7 6 5 4 3 2

Dedication

From Bobbi: To Todd and Kimberly

From Carol: To Charles

Acknowledgments

We are so grateful to Deb Rowden for planting the seed for this book and encouraging us to pursue its writing. Without her enthusiasm, this book would not have been written. We owe special thanks to Barbara Brackman for writing the foreword and for sharing her knowledge of tile quilts and quilt history in general. Special thanks also to our friends who fell in love with tile quilts along with us and have allowed us to share their quilts with you in this book: Georgann Eglinski, Ann Burgess, Kathe Dougherty, Nicki Listerman, Wendy Turnbull, Ann Rhode, Deb Rowden, Jackie Greenfield, Nan Losee, and the Glory Bee.

Bobbi would like to thank Jeanna Kimball and Marylou McDonald, from whom she learned a lot about appliqué. Carol would like to thank Bobbi, a pretty good appliqué teacher in her own right.

Our thanks to Bettina Havig and to Kimberly Ivey of the Colonial Williamsburg Foundation for providing images used in the history chapter; to Merikay Waldvogel for her energy and enthusiasm in locating the Olive/Alvo quilt; to Julie Silber for her generous help in tracing the Orange Peel quilt; to Kathy Ronsheimer for graciously scheduling our first presentation on tile quilts; and to Sarah Fayman for offering tile quilt workshops and generously sharing her tile quilt.

We are indebted to our editor, Liz Aneloski, for her prodigious problem-solving abilities and for all the sound advice she has given us. Thank you.

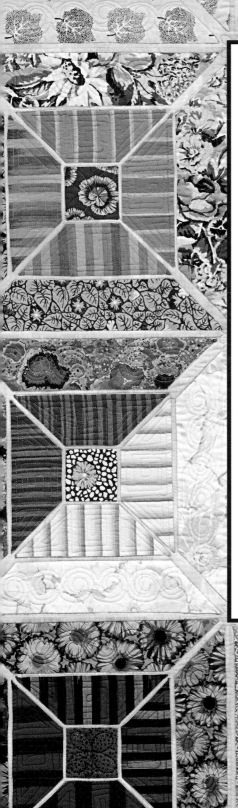

Contents

Foreword *by Barbara Brackman* 4

A Brief History of Tile Quilts 5

How to Make a Tile Quilt 10

Projects

    Lotus 19

    Birds in the Branches:
    Blue Sky Birds 22

    Birds in the Branches:
    Yellow Sky Birds 25

    Starry Orange Peel 27

    Art Deco Leaves 30

    Yukata Hydrangeas 33

    All in a Dream 37

Gallery of Contemporary Tile Quilts 41

Celebration of Collaboration 46

About the Authors 47

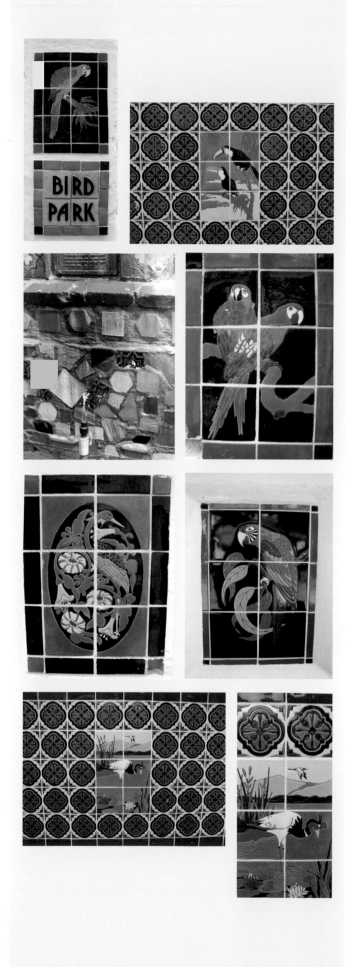

Foreword

Friendship and quilts are strongly linked. The making of this book is testimony to that tradition. Bobbi Finley and Carol Gilham Jones are close friends who do not live close by each other. Creating the quilts and writing the book have linked them through daily emails, frequent phone calls, and quilt blocks through the mail.

I also count myself as a close friend—a backdoor neighbor to Carol. It's been a pleasure to watch this book come together as a large circle of friends became caught up in Bobbi and Carol's enthusiasm, contributing ideas and quilts to this effort.

Carol and Bobbi love color and have a talent for using it in an innovative fashion. Both seem to have been born knowing how to take chances on palettes the rest of us can't imagine. When they discovered tile quilts they saw new opportunities to use fabric and color while reviving an almost forgotten part of quilt history.

As architecture fans, Carol and I have long been devotees of ceramic tile work, which adds brilliant color to cityscapes that might otherwise languish in gray or beige drabness. We've collected photos of glazed tiles and mosaics from Barcelona to the Watts Towers in Los Angeles. To the left, we offer a little travelogue from a recent vacation together, a weekend with our honorary extended family on California's Catalina Island, where the art deco tiles are part of the local architectural heritage.

This book is an invitation to look to your own architectural horizons for inspiration. After reading it you'll view appliqué in a fresh new way. Waking up under a tile quilt can make you think you're on vacation 365 days a year.

Barbara Brackman

A Brief History of Tile Quilts

We have shared an interest in tile quilts for many years and have often talked about collaborating in making one. As an introduction to our contemporary tile quilts, we want to provide a little history of the traditional tile quilts that we have loved looking at through the years and that have inspired us to finally make them ourselves.

Traditional tile quilts, also known by the names *Boston Pavement* and *Stonewall,* are a unique and somewhat obscure form of appliqué quilts. All the names are appropriate, as the quilts are constructed with small pieces of cotton fabric appliquéd in a random manner to a white background, leaving a narrow space between the pieces; this white space serves as the "grout" between the tiles or "mortar" between the pavers or stones. Tile quilt seems to be the predominant name applied to this style of quilt.

On some quilts, the small pieces of appliquéd fabric are all randomly shaped pieces, while other quilts contain recognizable cut-out images of animals and birds, people, flowers, celestial bodies, and other pictorial and geometric shapes combined with the randomly shaped pieces.

Very little documentation can be found on these quilts. Quilt historian Barbara Brackman found eleven examples when she discussed the topic in her online newsletter, *The Quilt Detective 2007.*[1] The earliest of the eleven quilts she found has a date range of 1865 to 1890, and the latest is dated circa 1900, so it is safe to say that these quilts were made in the last half of the nineteenth century. The quilts' origins are mostly attributed to New England (mainly Connecticut) or the greater northeastern area of the United States.

There is a theory that tile quilts were precursors to the fancy crazy quilts that were so popular in the early twentieth century. Like tile quilts, crazy quilts were also made with small pieces of fabric sewn in random patterns, but crazy quilts tended to be made from silks, velvets, ribbons, and other clothing and home furnishing fabrics, and were lavishly embellished. There are no grout spaces around the pieces. While this theory may be true, both styles may have developed independently.

There is another theory that these quilts originated in Britain as a style of Broderie Perse, also known as cut-out chintz appliqué. Early British quilts have been found that feature cut-out images and shapes appliquéd to a background fabric in which the patches form patterns that are random and chaotic rather than the more usual style of Broderie Perse, in which the cut-out chintz fabric creates a formal design of larger floral wreaths or bouquets. The random design may suggest tile quilts.

A tile quilt pattern was published in early editions of the Ladies' Art Company[2] catalog. Pattern #170 appeared in the 1908 catalog and was called *Stonewall.* The pattern was first printed in the 1898 catalog and is pictured in *Crazy Quilts*[3] by Cindy Brick. The block consisted of odd-shaped triangles to be appliquéd with narrow paths between them.

The name *Stonewall* coincides with the name of the earliest tile quilt we have discovered in various publications. It is found in *Quilts and Quiltmakers, Covering Connecticut.*[4] It was made by Florence Briggs Haviland of Sherman, Connecticut, and is dated circa

1865–1890. The quilt measures 80 inches by 90 inches. All of the twenty blocks consist of random shapes of multicolored prints and solids, with no pictorial images. On three sides is a pieced border of small Nine Patches set on point on a white background. It is suggested that the name comes from the many stones cleared from the land by the early Connecticut farmers who "created a patchwork landscape with the stone walls they built. This quilt is a tribute to those stone walls."[5]

A tile quilt called *Streets of Boston* is in the Shelburne Museum collection in Shelburne, Vermont. The quilt was made by two sisters from Nepaug, Connecticut—Augusta and Martha Kimberly, ages 11 and 14, respectively—for their older sister, Ellen May, age 23, as a wedding gift. This quilt has 25 full blocks with 5 partial blocks at the bottom. The center block has the initials "E.M.K." and the date "1873" appliquéd to the white background fabric. This is enclosed in an oval of blue print fabric and surrounded by randomly shaped tiles. In the center block of the top row is a star, and a double circle is in the center block in the bottom row. A catalog[6] of a 1997 exhibit in Japan of quilts from the Shelburne collection states that the center block represents Boston Common, the star indicates Fort Independence, and the double circle represents the Bunker Hill Monument, and that these symbols were common on nineteenth-century maps to mark historic sites. From the name, *Streets of Boston*, one might look at the quilt as a map of Boston, with the grout lines representing the streets of the city. Whether this was the Kimberly sisters' intended meaning or the caption writer's interpretation we can never know.[7] The quilt measures 80 inches by 76 inches and has no border.

A tile quilt in the collection of the Museum of Our National Heritage in Lexington, Massachusetts, has 100 blocks set 10 across and 10 down and has no border. Most of the blocks contain random shapes, but two blocks feature Masonic symbols and two others have single birds in the centers of the blocks with random shapes around the birds. This quilt measures 85 inches by 84 inches and dates from the last quarter of the nineteenth century. It is pictured in *Crazy Quilts*[8] by Penny McMorris.

A somewhat more orderly tile quilt is featured in *The Quilt Digest 4*.[9] This quilt is composed of 99 blocks, placed 9 across by 11 down, and measures 84 inches by 69 inches. The alternating blocks feature the same pattern of four kite-shaped

Streets of Boston tile quilt made by two young girls as a wedding gift for their older sister.
Photo courtesy of Shelburne Museum, Shelburne, Vermont

Detail of a somewhat more orderly tile quilt featuring cut-out images and alternating blocks with kite-shaped pieces.
Photo courtesy of Bettina Havig

"Hattie Burdick" tile quilt, International Quilt Study Center, University of Nebraska, Lincoln. 1997.007.0163

pieces—two each from one light and one dark fabric and placed diagonally opposite each other. Grout appears between the pieces on the inside, and a larger amount of background shows at the outside of the pieces, creating a more open appearance to the whole quilt. The other blocks are the usual random shapes with grout between the pieces. Some of these blocks have pictorial images of flowers, birds, and a windmill, and there is a sunflower in the center block. This quilt is dated circa 1875–1900 and placed in New England. It has no border.

The International Quilt Study Center (IQSC) in Lincoln, Nebraska, has two tile quilts in its collection. One is an unquilted top that was made by members of the Burdick family, probably in New London, Connecticut, circa 1876. It measures 81 inches by 80 inches and contains 30 blocks

plus 6 half-blocks on each side. In the block in the center of the third row from the top, letters spelling "HATTIE BURDICK" are found with grout around them. Also in that block is a cut-out cat and printed images of flowers and a bird. Other pictorial images, including a cross and a horseshoe, appear in other blocks, as well as randomly shaped pieces. The quilt has no border.

The second quilt in the IQSC collection was probably also made in Connecticut. It measures 83 inches by 78 inches and contains 25 blocks with random geometric shapes, including the cut-out letters "OEW" and the date "1900." This quilt also has no border.

Pictured in the *Quilt Engagement Calendar 1999*[10] is a "Crazy summer spread" circa 1880 that is definitely in the style of a tile quilt, as it has the usual grout around each of the random cut-out shapes. This quilt is made from predominantly brown printed fabrics, with many plaids and stripes. Rather than the usual block format, it appears to be made from three long pieces of fabric—with a wider one in the center and narrower ones at each side—as only two vertical seams are visible. Throughout the piece are many cut-out cats, birds, and a horse. This summer spread measures 82½ inches by 63 inches and has a binding but no border.

Another "summer spread" was exhibited at the Lincoln (Nebraska) Quilt Symposium in 1977. While definitely constructed as a tile quilt, with appliquéd cut-out shapes and grout between the pieces, it also varies from the usual block format as it is constructed as one whole piece. Most noticeable of the many images on this piece are the names "OLIVE" and "ALVO" and the date "1895." The maker (was it Olive?) was obviously very imaginative and filled the spread with many images, including several radiating fan and/or sun shapes, a ladder, a brick wall, a chain, a star and crescent moon, leaves, horseshoes, a bucket, crosses, hearts, a shoe, a sock, a turtle, a yellow house with a red door, a chair, stairs, and a zigzag, to name a few. There are also printed fabric pieces with images of

people, cats, butterflies, and birds. Some of the images suggest Log Cabin quilt blocks. The fabrics are both prints and solids of many colors, many with geometric patterns, and all finely stitched to the white background fabric. The quilt is 69 inches by 80 inches and is not backed or quilted but is finished with a light brown binding.

Colonial Williamsburg's Abby Aldrich Rockefeller Folk Art Museum in Williamsburg, Virginia, has a tile quilt that breaks the mold in several ways. It features sixteen blocks and a machine appliquéd border with an undulating vine of flowers and leaves on a white background. Only three of the tile quilts that we have found have borders, and this is the only one with an appliquéd border. Among the cut-out images of animals, birds, butterflies, and a cross is the image of a man with a black face leading a horse behind a fence. There is some embellishment with silk embroidery threads. The curators date this quilt to 1875–1910. The sixteen blocks contain appliquéd pieces cut from printed and solid cottons on a white background and the usual quarter-inch grout between the pieces. It has a red binding and measures 70 inches by 68 inches.

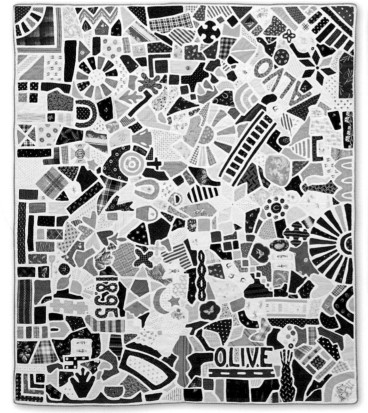

Tile quilt with appliquéd border, The Abby Aldrich Rockefeller Folk Art Museum, 2006.609.2

Olive and Alvo coverlet, dated 1895. A very imaginative work. Collection of Wendy Woodruff

The New England Quilt Museum has a wonderful quilt called *Boston Pavement*, which is featured in *The New England Quilt Museum Quilts*.[11] The maker is unknown but the quilt is attributed to Boston, Massachusetts, circa 1895. Five blocks wide and seven blocks long, it is made from multicolored prints and solids appliquéd on a cream background. Many of the cut-out pieces are printed flowers, animals, people (including a couple playing badminton), fans, a moon and star, birds, a horseshoe, and so on. This quilt measures 59½ inches by 81½ inches and has no border.

A tile quilt found in *The Quilt Engagement Calendar Treasury*[12] is attributed to Pennsylvania, circa 1900. It is five blocks wide and six blocks long and measures 76 inches by 64 inches. This quilt has blocks of a large orange-peel pattern with random pieces around the orange-peel shapes; these blocks alternate with the more usual blocks of all random shapes and pictorial elements. Many of the orange-peel shapes are cut from a chrome orange fabric, and there is a lot of chrome orange scattered throughout the blocks, along with green, red, pink, and blue. There are many stripes and plaids among the printed fabrics. Some of the alternating blocks contain star and moon shapes. The border consists of two strips of fabric, a pink inner strip and a green outer strip. When we made our first tile quilt, this is the quilt from which we drew our inspiration. You will find our quilt, *Starry Orange Peel*, pictured on page 27, followed by the project instructions on pages 28–29.

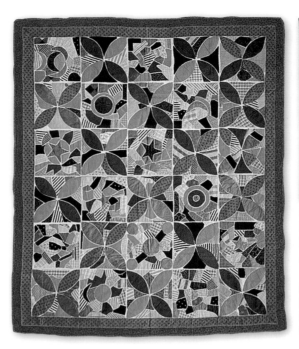

Boston Pavement tile quilt from Boston with many cut-out images, The New England Quilt Museum, 1988.05

Orange Peel tile quilt with stripped border
Photo courtesy of Julie Silber, The Quilt Complex, Albion, California

Since we began our search for historic tile quilts, we have come across a few more than the eleven we have discussed here. We hope more of these delightful creations will surface, and we hope you will be inspired to create your own version of a tile quilt.

ENDNOTES

1. Barbara Brackman, *The Quilt Detective: Clues in Pattern*, 2007, digital newsletter, #15.

2. Ladies Art Company. Founded in St. Louis by H.M. Brockstedt. It is credited as the first mail-order quilt pattern company. The date of publication of the first pattern is not yet known, but it was before an advertisement in 1895.

3. Cindy Brick, *Crazy Quilts: History, Techniques, Embroidery Motifs* (Voyageur Press, 2008), p. 51.

4. The Connecticut Quilt Search Project, *Quilts and Quiltmakers, Covering Connecticut* (Schiffer Publishing Ltd., 2002), p. 162.

5. Ibid.

6. *Quilts from the Shelburne Museum*, Japanese Exhibit Catalog, 1996, pp. 104–105.

7. Ibid. 1.

8. Penny McMorris, *Crazy Quilts* (Penguin Group [USA] Incorporated, 1984), p. 41.

9. *The Quilt Digest 4* (The Quilt Digest Press, 1986), p. 85.

10. Cyril I. Nelson, compiler, *Quilt Engagement Calendar 1999* (Penguin Studio, 1999), Plate 4.

11. Jennifer Gilbert, *The New England Quilt Museum Quilts* (C&T Publishing, 1999), p. 88.

12. Cyril I. Nelson & Carter Houck, *The Quilt Engagement Calendar Treasury* (E. P. Dutton, Inc., 1982), p. 90, plate 89.

How to Make a Tile Quilt

For a long time we had greatly admired historic tile quilts and often contemplated making one together. The question was—how? Trying to answer that question, we studied the earlier quilts and selected one we wanted to interpret. In designing, stitching, and completing our quilt, we developed a very simple method for making tile quilts using needle-turn appliqué. In contrast to some other forms of hand appliqué, our tile quilt technique eliminates any need to consider seam allowances, reverse images, or figure out where to place the appliqué pieces on the background fabric. Best of all, this technique produces exciting twenty-first-century quilts.

Here is the technique we used:

1. Choose a pattern or make a simple line-drawing pattern the size of the intended block.

2. Trace the pattern onto the dull side of freezer paper.

3. Cut the freezer paper apart along the pattern lines.

4. Iron each freezer-paper pattern piece onto the right side of the chosen fabric.

5. Cut each fabric shape right along the edge of the freezer paper.

6. Reassemble the pattern on a piece of background fabric.

7. Remove the freezer paper.

8. Baste the fabric shapes onto the background fabric.

9. Appliqué.

As the seam allowance on each fabric shape (tile) is turned under and sewn, a line of background fabric ("grout") is revealed. When the seam allowances on adjacent tile pieces have been turned under, the resulting line of grout will measure approximately ¼″–⅜″.

Do not be put off by the need to appliqué. If you love to appliqué, then a tile quilt is an ideal project for you. But even if you don't love to appliqué or don't consider yourself to be skilled at it, chances are you will enjoy the tile quilt process because it is not exacting. The tile-and-grout form is quite forgiving, and the inevitable deviations from strict uniformity in the grout add to the visual interest and appeal of a piece. And don't be concerned about stitching the thin points on some of the tile pieces; they will simply be cut off as you stitch to create blunter, more easily appliquéd shapes. Give hand appliqué a try— a tile block stitches up quickly, and the exciting result will bolster your confidence and stimulate your creativity. Refer to pages 13–15 for hand appliqué instructions.

If hand appliqué is not your idea of a pleasant way to spend your time, consider the possibility of machine appliqué using the instructions on page 16.

Another alternative to hand appliqué is fusible appliqué. Refer to pages 16–17 for fusible appliqué instructions.

Using the Patterns in This Book

The tile block patterns generally are 10″ square. The 10″ blocks work well for fusible appliqué and simpler blocks. You may prefer a larger format if you are doing hand appliqué. We recommend that you use 15″ blocks if you are making *Lotus* or *Starry Orange Peel* with hand appliqué because of the complexity of some of the blocks. To make 15″ blocks, enlarge the patterns 150% using a photocopy machine.

Choosing Fabrics

TILE FABRICS

The tile quilt technique, with its large and simple shapes, creates an ideal showcase for bold, contemporary fabrics. Interesting, large-scale prints are well suited for the tile pieces. If you've ever found yourself admiring some of the daring prints now available but wondering how to use them, a tile quilt is an ideal project for putting them to good use.

Contemporary fabrics that would jump-start any tile quilt

BACKGROUND FABRIC

Two factors are important to consider in selecting the background fabric: the color scheme and whether or not you want a solid background. If the colors or values of the block vary widely from one area to another, consider the possibility of using more than one background fabric and piecing the background. Many different background fabrics, including small- and large-scale prints, batiks, light and dark solids, plaids, and ikats, have been used in the quilts in this book. In each case, the selection reflects individual preference as well as the characteristics of the tile fabrics. Look for a color and texture that will enhance the palette rather than just provide a neutral background for it.

The background fabric of some blocks, in addition to furnishing the grout, is an important part of the design. *Lotus* (page 19), for example, includes several blocks in which areas of the background fabric frame and set off the principal shapes. Areas of exposed background fabric are designated on the patterns.

Needle-Turn Appliqué

Let's walk through the steps of the needle-turn appliqué tile technique using block C of *Lotus*. (The instructions for the entire project begin on page 20.)

Block C of *Lotus*

PREPARING THE APPLIQUÉ PIECES

1. From pattern pullout page P1, choose the pattern for block C of *Lotus*.

2. Place the freezer paper with the shiny side down on top of the pattern and trace the solid lines of the pattern onto the dull side of the freezer paper in pencil. (The dashed lines are for fusible appliqué.) Number the shapes to correspond to the numbers on the pattern.

Trace pattern on freezer paper and number pieces.

3. Refer to the pattern and audition fabrics by folding and placing them in the appropriate arrangement. Label each fabric with the corresponding piece number.

Audition fabrics.

4. Cut the freezer-paper pattern apart along the lines.

Cut on lines.

5. Iron each piece of freezer paper, shiny side down, onto the *right* side of the chosen fabric.

6. Cut each fabric shape *along the edge* of the freezer paper. *Do not add seam allowances.*

Cut fabric along edge of freezer paper.

7. Cut a piece of background fabric. Because the stitching usually draws in the background fabric, allow at least 1″ extra on each side of the pattern for squaring up the block after it is stitched. Thus, for a 10″ pattern, cut a square at least 12″ × 12″.

8. Reassemble the pattern pieces on the background fabric with the freezer paper on top and no spaces between the pieces.

Reassemble pattern pieces on background fabric.

9. Carefully remove the freezer paper.

Tip

Save the freezer paper patterns; they can be used repeatedly. If you aren't satisfied with a fabric choice, you can iron the freezer-paper pattern piece onto a different fabric and place it in the block.

10. Baste the fabric shapes onto the background fabric using a long running stitch to securely hold the fabric shapes on the background block while you appliqué. Baste far enough from the raw edge to allow for turning under the seam allowance.

Note

◇ We prefer thread basting, especially for the larger tile pieces, but you also may choose to hold the fabric shapes in place with water-soluble glue or fine appliqué pins.

Baste.

STITCHING THE APPLIQUÉ PIECES

1. Choose a thread color that matches the appliqué piece and cut a length no longer than 18″; longer pieces of thread tend to knot and fray. Knot the end of the thread.

Tip

There are a variety of appliqué needles on the market, including size 11 straw needles, which are long and very thin; size 10 milliners, which are not as long and thicker; or size 11 sharps. All work well and are favored by various appliqué teachers. Experiment until you find what works best for your hands.

2. Start stitching on the straightest edge of the appliqué piece. If you are right-handed, stitch counterclockwise; left-handers should stitch clockwise around the piece.

3. Holding the basted block in the hand opposite the hand holding the needle ("holding hand"), thumb on top and fingers underneath, begin by using the side of the threaded needle to turn under the seam allowance about ⅛″ on one of the tile pieces in the center of the block. It is important to use the side of the needle and not the point, which may shred the cut edge of the fabric, destroying the seam allowance. As you continue to stitch, you can use the point of the needle underneath the folded seam and away from the fold to adjust the seam if necessary, especially on curves.

Use side of needle to turn under edge of seam allowance.

4. Once the seam is folded under, hold it in place with the thumb of your holding hand on or just under the fold.

5. Bring the needle up from the back of the background fabric through the edge of the folded seam to the front of the piece, leaving the knot on the back. You've made the first stitch.

Bring needle up through folded seam.

6. Take the next stitch by inserting the needle straight down into the background fabric, next to the first stitch. Turn the needle and bring it back up through the background fabric and the edge of the fold as you did with the first stitch, about ⅛″ over from that first stitch. Keeping the needle straight as it goes down and back up through the fabric will help make sure the stitched edge lies flat. This may be awkward initially, but it is something to strive for. Aim for 7–9 stitches per inch in general. Points and concave areas may require tighter stitches.

Insert needle down next to stitch and come up through background and edge of fold.

Points

1. As you approach the point of an appliqué piece, with the seam turned under, stop at the place where the new seam will turn then take an extra stitch close to the last stitch.

2. Trim away any excess fabric under the seam. This is important in order for the point to lie as flat as possible, without a big lump.

Cut away excess fabric.

3. Cut off the point, leaving a ⅛″ seam allowance.

4. Hold the piece with the point up and use the side of the needle to turn under the seam allowance of the point. With the appliqué piece flat across the tip of the point, take a stitch right next to the last stitch.

5. Turn the piece in the direction of the next side to be stitched, and use the side of the needle to turn under the seam allowance. Continue stitching, with the stitches a little tighter at the beginning.

Concave Areas

In order for the piece to lie flat, it is important to clip into concave (inward) curves.

Make clips into the appliqué piece, ½″–1½″ apart, to within a few threads of where the seam will be folded under, clipping closer on tighter curves. If the curve is tight, take closer stitches in this area.

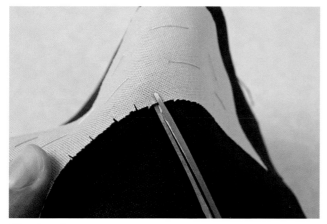

Clip edges of curve.

If your design contains tight inward points (V shapes), a little extra attention is required.

1. Clip into the bottom of the V as above.

2. Stop stitching about 2 stitches from the point. Turn the piece so the V is at the bottom.

3. Turn under the seam allowance on the opposite side from where you stopped stitching and at the bottom of the V. Do this by inserting the side of the needle on the edge of the fabric of the opposite side and "sweeping" it down and around, under the bottom of the V to the end of the stitches. Do this several times until you are sure the seam is turned under and there are no stray threads.

4. Now, take the next 1 or 2 stitches to the point.

5. At the point, take a deep stitch, 4 or 5 threads from the edge.

6. Take the next stitch by placing the point of the needle underneath the edge next to where the last stitch came up, bringing the needle up horizontally through the background and the edge of the seam and pulling the stitch tight. This will give you a nice sharp inverted point.

7. Continue stitching along the other side, with the first few stitches a little closer together.

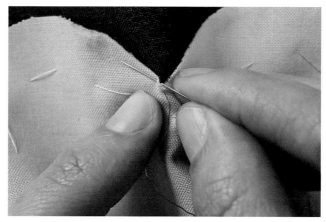

Insert needle just under edge, after deep stitch.

8. Finish off the stitching by drawing the needle to the back of the piece. Take a small stitch in the background fabric in the seam and wrap the thread around the needle before drawing it out, making a knot. You may want to bury the thread by drawing the needle between the background and the appliqué piece, bringing it up an inch or so away, and then cutting the thread. The back of your work will look neater, although of course it will be covered when quilted, but it also limits the risk of the tail of a dark thread being visible under a light background after it has become a quilt.

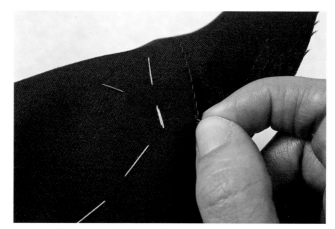

Insert needle between background and appliquéd piece.

Note

We do not cut out the background fabric behind the appliqué, in order to maintain the straight of grain of the background fabric. The appliqué pieces may be on the bias, which we feel weakens the piece if the straight-of-grain area is removed.

Machine Appliqué

1. Prepare the appliqué pieces referring to Preparing the Appliqué Pieces on page 12, Steps 1–9.

2. Press a ⅛″ seam allowance to the wrong side of the fabric on each piece. Clip concave curves as necessary for the seam allowance to lie flat. (Refer to the photo in Concave Areas, page 15.)

3. Position and pin the appliqué pieces securely to the background fabric.

4. Use an overlock or hem stitch with a very short stitch length and width and monofilament thread on the top and in the bobbin.

5. Stitch right along the edge of the appliqué piece. The straight stitches will pass along the outside of the tile shape without penetrating it; the intermittent zigzag stitches will go into the tile shape and tack it to the background fabric.

Tip

If you have difficulty machine appliquéing sharp points, stop machine stitching before reaching the points and hand tack them. Then continue stitching.

Fusible Appliqué

The tile block patterns have a dashed line ⅛″ inside the solid line for each pattern piece. These dashed lines are the tracing and cutting lines for fusible appliqué.

In order for the finished block design to match the original pattern, a reverse of each pattern shape must be made.

1. For each pattern template, trace the dashed line of the shape onto a piece of paper. On this template, mark the letter or number label shown on the pattern. Cut out on the line.

2. Place the paper template, label side down, on the paper side of the fusible adhesive, and trace around the template. This gives you the reversed pattern you need. Cut out the fusible adhesive with about 1″ extra around the marked line.

3. Cut a piece of the selected fabric slightly larger than the fusible adhesive.

4. Fuse the adhesive to the wrong side of the fabric, following the manufacturer's instructions.

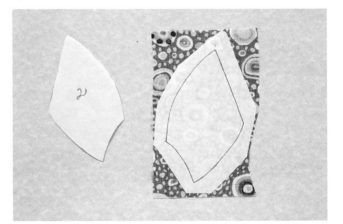

Fuse reversed template (no number visible) to wrong side of fabric.

5. Cut the fabric and fusible web on the marked line.

6. Peel off the paper backing. A thin film of adhesive will remain on the back side of the fabric.

7. After all the pattern pieces are fused to their appropriate fabrics, arrange them on the right side of the background, leaving space—the "grout"—between the tile pieces, and fuse in place.

8. Blanket stitch, zigzag stitch, or straight stitch by machine around the edge of each appliqué shape. Another alternative is to blanket stitch by hand around the edge using 2 strands of embroidery floss or quilting thread.

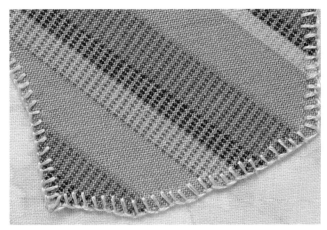

Blanket stitch

Zigzag stitch

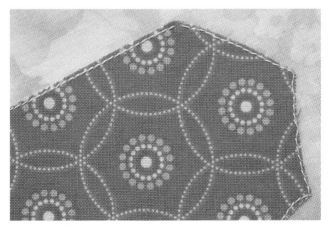

Straight stitch

Finishing the Quilt

SQUARING UP THE BLOCKS

1. When the appliquéd blocks have been completed, press them wrong side up on a washcloth or towel.

2. Square up each block and trim to the size required for the pattern, adding ½″ to each dimension.

Example: A 10″ finished block would be trimmed to 10½″ × 10½″. The area covered by finished tile pieces measures approximately 9¾″ × 9¾″. With the blocks seamed together, approximately ¼″ of background fabric will appear between a tile piece on the edge of one block and a tile piece on the edge of the neighboring block. This creates a line of grout between the blocks.

Tip

Be careful when trimming the blocks. Measure them all first. When the blocks are trimmed, there should be approximately ⅜″ of background fabric ("grout") around all the edges. If this means the blocks must be trimmed to a different size than specified, trim all the blocks to the size of the largest one.

QUILTING

The quilts in this book have been quilted by hand and by home and longarm sewing machines. The quilting objective should be to enrich the overall look without adding significant additional texture. For this reason, quilting thread that matches the background fabric is a good choice. Many of the quilts were quilted in the grout between the tile pieces, avoiding stitching on the tile pieces. The type and amount of quilting is your choice.

Simplifying the Patterns

Some of the patterned tile blocks are simpler than others. The blocks with a larger number of tile pieces pose a greater challenge for hand appliqué than do the simpler blocks. If you prefer to simplify your sewing, reduce the number of pieces in a pattern by eliminating some of the lines between adjoining pattern pieces. You may also choose to eliminate some of the edge pieces, leaving more background exposed.

Notice how *Lotus* block C was simplified by enlarging the pieces near the center and removing some of the pieces nearer the edge, leaving more of the background exposed and reducing the number of pattern pieces from 23 to 9.

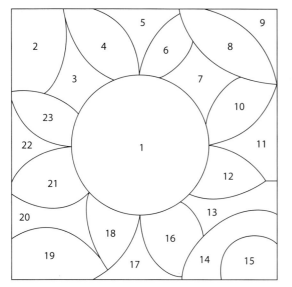

Original pattern

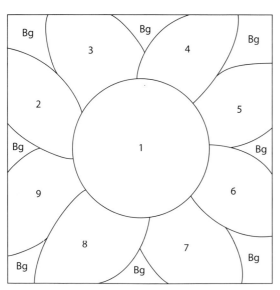

Simplified pattern; Bg = Background fabric

Creating Your Own Designs

The directness of the tile quilt technique provides an opportunity for designing your own tile quilts. A pattern is a simple line drawing.

1. Cut a piece of paper the intended finished size of the block.

To determine the size of the block, consider how large you want the finished quilt to be, how many blocks you want to make, the optimum size for the shapes you are using, and the scale of the pattern in the fabrics.

2. Draw the principal shapes in pencil.

Use large, simple geometric shapes or simple images, such as stars or birds, that are readily recognizable from their silhouettes. The drawing should extend all the way to the edges of the paper.

3. Draw lines defining shapes to break up the space surrounding the principal shapes.

Very softly curved lines create simple, easily appliquéd pieces. Limit the number of surrounding shapes; a good rule of thumb is to aim for approximately the same number of total shapes as inches on a side of the pattern. Number the pieces.

4. Proceed as described for the tile quilt technique.

Inspired to make a tile quilt? We certainly hope so. Start with one of the projects in this book or design your own using the simple line-drawing method we have described. We encourage you to get in touch with your creativity. Enjoy!

Lotus

Lotus, Bobbi Finley, Williamsburg, Virginia, 2008

SIZE: 30½″ × 30½″ (45½″ × 45½″)
BLOCKS: 10″ × 10″ (15″ × 15″) finished

Lotus is a sumptuous garden, designed to show off the large lace and floral motifs of the focus fabric on which each block is built. The circular motifs are used in many ways—centered, off-center, solo, in multiples, and mixed within the same block. The large-scale prints used in the tile pieces accentuate the abundance, and even the background fabric in this fantastic garden is floral. You would look in vain for a straight-sided tile shape in any of the blocks, so stripes and geometric prints provide an invigorating contrast.

Like many nineteenth-century tile quilts, *Lotus* is complete without a border. It is bound with the background fabric and backed with the lotus motif fabric.

The primary instructions for this quilt and the patterns are based on 10″ blocks. The 10″ blocks work well for fusible appliqué. You may prefer a larger format, and, in fact, we recommend using 15″ blocks if you are making this quilt with hand appliqué. Dimensions and fabric requirements for 15″ blocks are given in parentheses. For the 15″ blocks, enlarge the patterns 150%.

Fabric Requirements

PRINT: 1⅛ (2½) yards for background fabric

FOCUS FABRIC: 1 yard (approximately) for cut-out motifs/images; 9 large, 7 medium, and 5 small

STRIPE, GEOMETRIC, AND LARGE-SCALE FLORAL FABRICS: scraps, fat eighths, or fat quarters of 15 (25) fabrics (minimum) for tile pieces around focus images

BACKING: 1⅛ (3¼) yards

BATTING: 34″ × 34″ (53″ × 53″)

BINDING: ⅓ (½) yard for straight-grain double-fold 2″-wide binding

Lotus features large, round lace and floral printed fabric images. Each block is constructed around one or more of the circles.

Fabrics with large printed images suitable for incorporating into tile blocks

Design Hint

If you are using stripes, plaids, or geometric prints, you may want to pay attention to the direction the design is placed.

Tile Blocks

The patterns for the blocks are on pattern pullout pages P1–P2. The patterns are designated A through I, beginning with the block in the upper left and proceeding horizontally across the rows, and ending with the block in the lower right. Refer to pages 13–15 for needle-turn appliqué, page 16 for machine appliqué, or pages 16–17 for fusible appliqué techniques.

A	B	C
D	E	F
G	H	I

Letter designations for tile blocks

The complete circles in the patterns represent printed-fabric-image tile pieces in *Lotus*. You may choose whether or not to use printed fabric images in any or all of the pattern circles.

Tip

If your printed fabric image is not absolutely circular, cut it as if it were in order to make it conform to the pattern

1. Cut 9 squares 12″ × 12″ (17″ × 17″) of background fabric.

2. Prepare the pieces and appliqué the blocks.

3. Trim the blocks (page 17).

4. Sew the blocks together.

Finish the Quilt

1. Layer and baste.

2. Quilt. Initially, *Lotus* was hand quilted simply in the grout between the tile pieces. On second look, the large motifs seemed to call for more definition, so quilting was added to various elements in the motifs.

3. Bind.

Block I quilting

Birds in the Branches: Blue Sky Birds

Blue Sky Birds, Carol Gilham Jones and Georgann Eglinski, Lawrence, Kansas, 2008

SIZE: 40¼″ × 20¼″ (59¾″ × 29¾″)
BIRD BLOCKS: 10″ × 10″ (15″ × 15″) finished
BORDER CORNER BLOCKS: 4⅞″ × 4⅞″ (7⅛″ × 7⅛″) finished

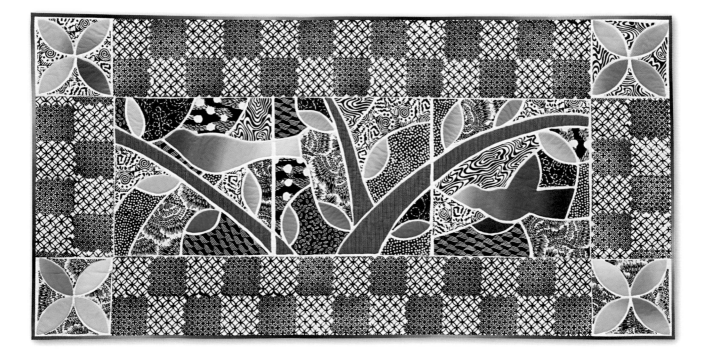

In this quilt, several blocks connect to form a scene. Pictorial images in the central blocks and geometric patterns in the corner blocks of the border combine for visual appeal. Shared shapes and colors unite the central blocks and the border. The birds, leaves, and orange-peel shapes are rendered in clear, bright color gradations; blue-and-white batiks of many different patterns create an interesting sky and backgrounds for the orange-peel shapes. The background fabric is white. The border strips are a blue-and-white batik with the appearance of blue-and-white geometric tiles, which adds a visual pun to this quilt.

The primary instructions for this quilt and the patterns are based on 10″ bird blocks. You may prefer to work on a somewhat larger scale if you are doing hand appliqué, are using large-scale prints, or simply want your finished quilt to be larger than the dimensions produced with 10″ bird blocks. Dimensions and fabric requirements for 15″ bird blocks are given in parentheses. For 15″ bird blocks and correspondingly larger border corner blocks, enlarge the patterns 150%.

See page 25 for an alternative color scheme and border treatment for the bird blocks.

Fabric Requirements

LIGHT: ⅔ (1⅓) yard(s) for background fabric for bird and border corner blocks

BLUE-AND-WHITE BATIKS: 8 fat quarters, fat eighths, or scraps for sky and border corner blocks

GREENS AND BLUE-GREENS: ¼ yard total for leaves and border corner blocks

ORANGES AND CORALS: ¼ yard total for birds and border corner blocks

BROWN: ¼ yard for branches

BLUE-AND-WHITE CHECKERBOARD BATIK: 1 (1½) yard(s) for borders

BACKING: 1⅜ (2) yards

BATTING: 44″ × 24″ (64″ × 34″)

BINDING: ⅓ (½) yard for straight-grain double-fold 2″-wide binding

Tile Blocks

The patterns for the bird blocks and border corner blocks are on pattern pullout pages P2 and P4. Refer to pages 13–15 for needle-turn appliqué, page 16 for machine appliqué, or pages 16–17 for fusible appliqué techniques.

Bird Blocks

1. Cut 3 squares 12″ × 12″ (17″ × 17″) of background fabric.

2. Prepare the pieces and appliqué each of the 3 blocks, varying the colors of the leaves and the birds.

3. Trim the blocks (page 17).

4. Sew the blocks together.

Design Hint

The "grout" in a tile block generally functions as negative space, but in special circumstances it can become visually positive, as in the legs of the perching bird in the block on the previous page. Instead of being appliquéd, the legs are suggested by lines of background fabric between pieces of the sky fabrics.

Border Corner Blocks

1. Cut 4 squares 7″ × 7″ (9½″ × 9½″) of background fabric.

2. Prepare the pieces and appliqué the 4 corner blocks, varying the colors of the orange-peel shapes.

3. Trim the blocks (page 17).

Border

1. To determine the top and bottom border length, measure the seamed bird blocks horizontally from one side to the other.

2. To determine the top and bottom border width, measure from top to bottom of the border corner blocks.

3. Cut 2 strips to these measurements.

4. Sew the strips to the top and bottom of the seamed bird blocks.

5. To determine the side border length, measure from seam to seam along the side edge of the bird blocks and add ½″.

6. The width of the side border strips will be the same as the width of the top and bottom border strips.

7. Cut 2 strips to these measurements.

8. Sew a border corner block to each end of the strips.

9. Sew the strips to the quilt, matching the seams.

Finish the Quilt

1. Layer and baste.

2. Quilt. This version of *Birds in the Branches* is hand quilted. Like the appliqué, the quilting combines pictorial and geometric elements. The birds, branches, leaves, and orange-peel shapes are quilted close to the appliquéd pieces to give them definition. All other quilting follows the grid of the border fabric. In the bird blocks, the grid quilting crisscrosses the tile pieces. This photograph of the back of the quilt shows the quilting scheme.

3. Bind.

Design Hint

The shaded-color binding moves the viewer's eye around the quilt.

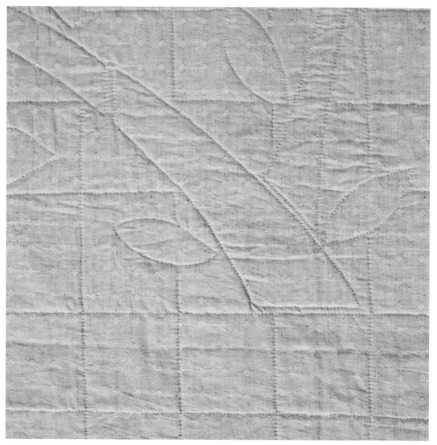

Quilting scheme combining pictorial and geometric elements

Birds in the Branches: Yellow Sky Birds

Yellow Sky Birds, Carol Gilham Jones and Georgann Eglinski, Lawrence, Kansas;
machine quilted by Shirley Greenhoe, Missoula, Montana, 2008

SIZE: 34½″ × 14½″ (51½″ × 21½″)
BIRD BLOCKS: 10″ × 10″ (15″ × 15″) finished

Quite a different look results from an alternative color scheme and
narrower, pieced border. In this example the background fabric is solid
yellow-green, the sky is pale yellow batiks and dots, the branches are
a very dark batik with a leaf pattern, the leaves are green and greenish
batiks, and the birds are red batiks. The light halves of the half-square
triangle units in the border are yellow-green and pale yellow; the dark
halves are the branch, leaf, and bird fabrics.

The primary instructions for this quilt and the patterns are based on 10″ bird blocks. If you prefer to work on a larger scale, dimensions and fabric requirements for 15″ bird blocks are given in parentheses where they vary from the 10″ block. For the 15″ bird blocks, enlarge the patterns 150%.

Fabric Requirements

YELLOW-GREEN: ⅝ (1⅓) yard(s) for background fabric for bird blocks and border

PALE YELLOW BATIKS AND DOTS: 3 fat quarters for sky and border

GREEN AND GREENISH BATIKS: 3 fat quarters for leaves and border

RED BATIK: 1 fat quarter for birds and border

DARK BATIK: 1 fat quarter for branches and border

BACKING: ⅝ (1⅞) yard(s)

BATTING: 38″ × 18″ (59″ × 25″)

BINDING: ¼ (⅜) yard for straight-grain double-fold 2″-wide binding

Tile Blocks

The patterns for the bird blocks are on pattern pullout pages P2 and P4. Refer to pages 13–15 for needle-turn appliqué, page 16 for machine appliqué, or pages 16–17 for fusible appliqué techniques.

Bird Blocks

1. Cut 3 squares 12″ × 12″ (17″ × 17″) of background fabric.

2. Prepare the pieces and appliqué each of the 3 blocks, varying the colors of the leaves.

3. Trim the blocks (page 17) to 10½″ × 10½″ (15½″ × 15½″). This quilt has a pieced border. In order for the border to fit, the blocks must be trimmed to these exact measurements.

4. Sew the blocks together.

Border

1. Cut 22 light and 22 dark squares 2⅞″ × 2⅞″ (3⅞″ × 3⅞″).

2. Cut each square in half diagonally to make 2 triangles.

3. Sew a light triangle to a dark triangle.

Sew light triangle to dark triangle.

4. Repeat to make 44 units.

5. Sew 15 units into a row. Make 2.

Sew 15 units into a row.

6. Sew 7 units into a row, with the seventh unit turned 90 degrees. Make 2.

Sew 7 units into a row, with seventh unit turned 90 degrees.

7. Sew the long rows to the top and bottom of the bird blocks.

8. Sew the short rows to the sides of the quilt. Note the orientation of the light/dark triangles.

Quilt assembly

Finish the Quilt

1. Layer and baste.

2. Quilt. This version of *Birds in the Branches* is machine quilted. The free swing and flow of repeated curves add rhythm and texture to the subtle surface patterns of the batiks and small dots.

3. Bind.

Starry Orange Peel

Starry Orange Peel, Bobbi Finley, Williamsburg, Virginia,
and Carol Gilham Jones, Lawrence, Kansas, 2007,
from the collection of Sarah Fayman

SIZE: 38″ × 38″ (57″ × 57″)
BLOCKS: 10″ × 10″ (15″ × 15″) finished

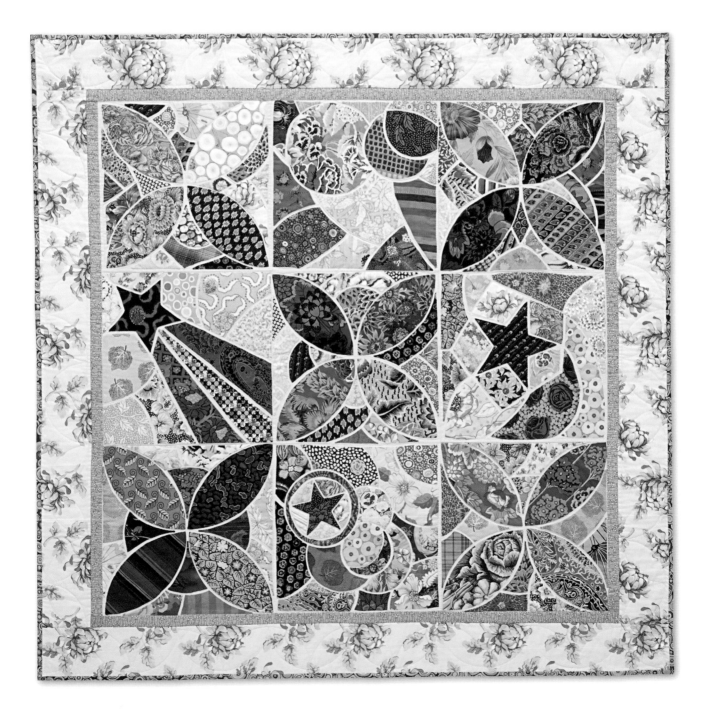

It's obvious that our inspiration for our first tile quilt, *Starry Orange Peel,* was the *Orange Peel* tile quilt of more than a century ago (page 9). What was it we found so tremendously appealing about the earlier quilt? We believe it was the combination of two important design elements: a strong geometric organizing principle and simple pictorial images. In making our quilt, we retained both the striking diagonal geometry and the fanciful depictions of celestial bodies.

Orange Peel block I

Star block F

We used bold, large-scale prints to breathe new life into the traditional form, and we chose fabrics with clear, fresh palettes. By selecting clear colors and avoiding grayed ones, we were able to include a great variety

of prints that work well together in a truly polychromatic color scheme. Given the colorful contemporary prints we favored for the tile pieces, we opted for the relative calm of a solid, soft yellow for the background fabric. The print of the outer border shares the large scale of many of the prints in the tile pieces.

The primary instructions for this quilt and the patterns are based on 10″ blocks. The 10″ blocks work well for fusible appliqué. You may prefer a larger format, and, in fact, we recommend using 15″ blocks if you are making this quilt with hand appliqué. Dimensions and fabric requirements for 15″ blocks are given in parentheses. To modify the patterns for 15″ blocks, enlarge them 150% on a photocopier.

Fabric Requirements

LIGHT: 1¼ (2½) yards for background fabric

PRINTS: ¼ yard each of a wide variety of fabrics for tile pieces

LIGHT BLUE: ¼ (¼) yard for inner border

PRINT: ⅝ (1) yard for outer border

BACKING: 1⅓ (3⅞) yards

BATTING: 42″ × 42″ (65″ × 65″)

BINDING: ⅜ (½) yard for straight-grain double-fold 2″-wide binding

Tile Blocks

The patterns for the tile blocks are on pattern pullout page P3. The patterns are designated A through I, beginning with the block in the upper left and proceeding horizontally across the rows, and ending with the block in the lower right. Refer to pages 13–15 for needle-turn appliqué, page 16 for machine appliqué, or pages 16–17 for fusible appliqué techniques.

A	B	C
D	E	F
G	H	I

Letter designations for tile blocks

There is a pattern for each of the celestial blocks B, D, F, and H. For the Orange Peel blocks, there are 2 patterns. One is for the Orange Peel block in the lower left corner of the quilt, G; it has a large circle in the center of the block. The other is for the other 4 Orange Peel blocks, A, C, E, and I. The orange-peel shapes in each of those 4 blocks are the same; in the quilt shown on page 27, the other tile shapes in each of those blocks are subtly different from the tile shapes in each of the other 3 blocks.

There are two ways you can proceed:

- You can use patterns A, C, E, and I on pattern pullout page P3 for each of the 4 blocks. In this case, the tile shapes in each of the blocks will be the same, but you can vary the appearance of the blocks through your choice and placement of fabrics.

- Or, you can actually vary the tile shapes in the blocks by using the pattern for 1 block and then drawing your own softly curving lines to divide up the space outside the orange-peel shapes for the other 3 blocks.

1. Cut 9 squares 12″ × 12″ (17″ × 17″) of background fabric.

2. Prepare the pieces and appliqué each of the 9 blocks, varying the colors and patterns of the tile shapes.

3. Trim the blocks (page 17).

4. Sew the blocks together.

Borders

Inner Border

1. To determine the top and bottom inner border length, measure the seamed blocks horizontally from one side to the other.

2. Cut 2 strips 1⅛″ wide × the measurement from Step 1. (For a quilt made with 15″ blocks, cut 3 strips 1½″ wide and seam together to make 2 strips 1½″ wide × the measurement from Step 1.)

3. Sew the strips to the top and bottom of the seamed tile blocks.

4. To determine the side inner border length, measure the quilt vertically from top to bottom (including the inner borders that were added in Step 3).

5. Cut 2 strips 1⅛″ wide × the measurement from Step 4. (For a quilt made with 15″ blocks, cut 3 strips 1½″ wide, and seam together to make 2 strips 1½″ wide × the measurement from Step 4.)

6. Sew the strips to the sides of the quilt.

Outer Border

1. To determine the top and bottom outer border length, measure the quilt (with the inner borders added) horizontally from one side to the other.

2. Cut 2 strips 3⅝″ wide × the measurement from Step 1. (For a quilt made with 15″ blocks, cut 3 strips 5¼″ wide, and seam together to make 2 strips 5¼″ wide × the measurement from Step 1.)

3. Sew the strips to the top and bottom of the quilt.

4. To determine the side outer border length, measure the quilt vertically from top to bottom (including the outer borders that were added in Step 3).

5. Cut 2 strips 3⅝″ wide × the measurement from Step 4. (For a quilt made with 15″ blocks, cut 3 strips 5¼″ wide, and seam together to make 2 strips 5¼″ wide × the measurement from Step 4.)

6. Sew the strips to the sides of the quilt.

Finish the Quilt

1. Layer and baste.

2. Quilt. We hand quilted *Starry Orange Peel* in the grout between the tile pieces and in the seams of the inner border. In the outer border quilting we echoed the orange-peel shapes of the tile blocks, rocking them back and forth along the length of each side.

3. Bind.

Art Deco Leaves

Art Deco Leaves, Carol Gilham Jones, Georgann Eglinski, and Deb Rowden, Lawrence, Kansas; machine quilted by Shirley Greenhoe, Missoula, Montana, 2008

SIZE: 31¾″ × 31¾″

LEAF BLOCKS: 10″ × 10″ finished

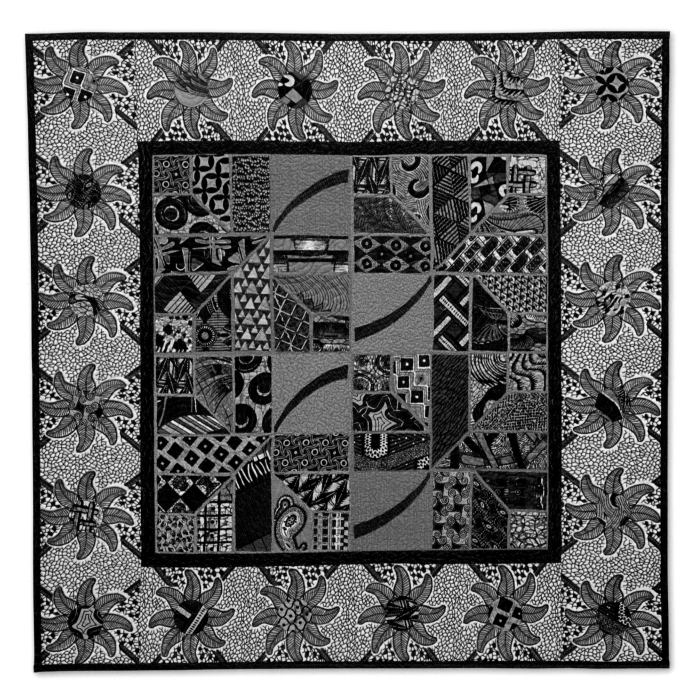

The surprising combination of an art deco leaf form and African fabrics enlivens this quilt. The highly stylized leaf is repeated four times—two leaves pointing up and to the right, and two leaves pointing down and to the left. With this configuration, the curved stems, which contrast with the straight-sided tile pieces of the leaf blade, draw the viewer's eye to the center of the quilt. The leaves and the border are tied together by the circles of fabrics used in the leaves appliquéd onto the printed floral motifs of the border.

Fabrics from center of quilt are repeated in circles on border appliqué.

Fabric Requirements

MEDIUM BROWN: ¾ yard of 1 fabric or ⅜ yard each of 2 fabrics for background fabric

AFRICAN OR OTHER ETHNIC FABRICS: ¼ yard each of a variety of fabrics for leaf pieces

DARK PRINT: ¼ yard for stems

PRINT: ¼ yard for inner border

AFRICAN OR OTHER ETHNIC FABRIC: ¾ yard for outer border

BACKING: 1⅛ yards

BATTING: 36″ × 36″

BINDING: ⅓ yard for straight-grain double-fold 2″-wide binding

Design Hint

Two different background fabrics, both small prints that read as solids, were used for the background fabrics in the leaf blocks. By mixing and matching the background fabrics of the tile blocks, you can increase their visual impact.

Note

The inner border and the binding are made from the same fabric in this project, *Art Deco Leaves*.

Tile Blocks

The pattern for the leaf block is on pattern pullout page P4. Refer to pages 13–15 for needle-turn appliqué, page 16 for machine appliqué, or pages 16–17 for fusible appliqué techniques.

The arcs of the leaf stems stand out against the exposed background fabric, which functions as part of the design. The areas intended to be background fabric, rather than a tile fabric, are designated on the pattern.

1. Cut 4 squares 12″ × 12″ of background fabric.

2. Prepare the pieces and appliqué each of the 4 blocks, scattering repetitions of the ethnic prints and eye-catching colors throughout the blocks.

3. Trim the blocks (page 17).

4. Sew the blocks together with the stems in the middle, the 2 leaf blocks on the right pointing toward the upper right corner, and the 2 leaf blocks on the left pointing toward the lower left corner. Refer to the photo on page 30 for placement.

Borders

Inner Border

1. To determine the top and bottom inner border length, measure the seamed blocks horizontally from one side to the other.

2. Cut 2 strips 1⅛″ wide × the measurement from Step 1.

3. Sew the strips to the top and bottom of the seamed blocks.

4. To determine the side inner border length, measure the quilt vertically from top to bottom (including the inner border that was just added).

5. Cut 2 strips 1⅛″ wide × the measurement from Step 4.

6. Sew the strips to the sides of the quilt.

Outer Border

The leaf and border elements of the quilt were harmonized by appliquéing circles of leaf fabrics on the border motifs. Other means of tying the leaves and border together might include using the border fabric in the leaves, using one or more leaf fabrics for border corner blocks, or using both.

> *Tip*
>
> If you are doing appliqué on the borders, cut the strips and complete the appliqué stitching before sewing the border strips onto the quilt in order to decrease the bulk of fabric involved in your handwork.

1. To determine the top and bottom outer border length, measure the quilt horizontally from one side to the other (including the inner borders).

2. Cut 2 strips 5½″ wide × the measurement from Step 1.

3. Sew the strips to the top and bottom of the quilt.

4. To determine the side outer border length, measure the quilt vertically from top to bottom (including the outer border that was just added).

5. Cut 2 strips 5½″ wide × the measurement from Step 4.

6. Sew the strips to the sides of the quilt.

Finish the Quilt

1. Layer and baste.

2. Quilt. The stylized tile leaves are quilted with a naturalistic leaf motif that has fluidly curving lines representing the veins of the leaf blades. The border is quilted in an overall pattern of echoing curves and spirals.

3. Bind.

Yukata Hydrangeas

Yukata Hydrangeas, Carol Gilham Jones, Lawrence, Kansas;
machine quilted by Shirley Greenhoe, Missoula, Montana, 2008

SIZE: 47¹¹⁄₁₆″ × 47¹¹⁄₁₆″ (71⅛″ × 71⅛″)
MEDALLION BLOCKS: 10″ × 10″ (15″ × 15″) finished
BORDER AND CORNER BLOCKS: 9⁷⁄₁₆″ × 9⁷⁄₁₆″ (14⅛″ × 14⅛″) finished

Delicious colors and patterns unify Broderie Perse, tile technique, and piecing in this medallion quilt. The center diamond is formed by four tile blocks set on point. The tile pieces in each of the tile blocks are arranged around a circle of pale pink background fabric that frames a bouquet of hydrangeas. The hydrangeas are printed images cut from Japanese cotton fabric.

Block detail of hydrangeas

In the setting triangles, a woven stripe radiates out from the center diamond. In the border, tile blocks combine with pieced blocks that repeat the circle motif. The tile blocks in the border corners are like those of the medallion but are not on point. Three pieced circle blocks make up each border strip.

The primary instructions for this quilt and the patterns are based on 10″ medallion blocks and 9⁷⁄₁₆″ border blocks. If you prefer to work on a somewhat larger scale, dimensions and fabric requirements for 15″ medallion blocks and 14⅛″ border blocks are given in parentheses. For the larger blocks, enlarge the patterns 150%.

Fabric Requirements

LIGHT: 1¼ (2⅛) yards for background fabric for medallion and border corners

STRIPE: ⅝ (1⅜) yard(s) for setting triangles

LARGE FLORAL PRINT: 8 bouquets for central bouquets in medallion and border corner tile blocks

Note

◊ Several different floral motifs may be used to add visual interest; the printed fabric images should be roughly 4″–8″ (6″–14″) in diameter. Several floral motifs may be combined to make a bouquet. You will need yardage sufficient to yield 8 bouquets.

PRINTS: ¼ yard each of a variety of fabrics that complement the floral motifs for tile pieces and pieced border blocks

BACKING: 3⅓ (4⅝) yards

BATTING: 55″ × 55″ (79″ × 79″)

BINDING: ½ (⅝) yard for straight-grain double-fold 2″-wide binding

Design Hint

Use some tile block background fabric in the pieced circles to better integrate the pieced and appliqué blocks.

Tile Blocks

The patterns for the tile blocks are on pattern pullout page P4. There is a pattern for the medallion tile blocks and a pattern for the border corner tile blocks. Note that the border corner blocks are slightly smaller than the medallion blocks. Refer to pages 13–15 for needle-turn appliqué, page 16 for machine appliqué, or pages 16–17 for fusible appliqué techniques.

The tile shapes in each of the 4 tile blocks that make up the medallion diamond are subtly different from each other. There are two ways you can proceed:

- You can use the pattern on the pullout for each of the medallion blocks. In this case, the tile shapes in each of the medallion blocks will be the same, but you can vary the appearance of the blocks through your choice and placement of fabrics.

- Or, you can actually vary the tile shapes in the medallion blocks by using the pattern for 1 block and drawing your own softly curving lines between the outer square line and the inner circle line for the other blocks.

Likewise, the tile shapes in each of the 4 border corner blocks are different from each other. Either of the two methods described for the tile shapes in the medallion blocks can be used for those in the border corner blocks.

Some of the bouquets extend beyond the area of exposed background fabric into the tile shapes, adding visual interest by breaking the circle boundary.

Detail of bouquet extending beyond circle of exposed background fabric

The patterns for the tile blocks, however, are drawn as if the bouquets will fit entirely within the circle of background fabric. If any of the bouquets overlap the tile shapes, you can easily adjust the pattern to fit your need. Where a part or parts of a bouquet overlap the tile shapes, pay particular attention to Step 5 in the following section.

Incorporating the Bouquets into the Pattern

1. Select bouquets from the large floral print. If the bouquets vary in size, select larger ones for the medallion blocks than for the border corner blocks.

2. Cut out a bouquet. Allow a generous ⅛" outside the image to turn under for needle-turn or machine appliqué or cut out the finished shape for fusible appliqué. If the outline of the bouquet is more complicated than you want to stitch, simplify it as you cut.

3. Photocopy the bouquet, and cut out the photocopied image.

4. Repeat Steps 1–3 for each different bouquet.

5. Center the photocopied image on the pattern. Position a large bouquet so it extends beyond the circle of background fabric as necessary.

6. Glue the cut-out image on the pattern or draw around it to create a guide for appliquéing.

Medallion Blocks

1. Cut 4 squares 12″ × 12″ (17″ × 17″) of background fabric.

2. Prepare the pieces and appliqué each of the 4 blocks, varying the colors and patterns of the tile shapes. Appliqué the bouquets to the blocks using the glued or drawn image as a guide.

3. Trim the blocks (page 17) to 10½″ × 10½″ (15½″ × 15½″). This quilt has a pieced border. In order for the border to fit, the blocks must be trimmed to these exact measurements.

4. Sew the blocks together.

Design Hint

Because the background fabric is cut on grain and will not be cut away behind the tile shapes, the tile pieces do not need to be cut on grain. Thus, you may use directional fabrics as you please.

Border Corner Blocks

1. Cut 4 squares 11½″ × 11½″ (16″ × 16″) of background fabric.

2. Make each of the 4 blocks, varying the colors and patterns of the tile shapes. Appliqué the bouquets to the blocks using the glued or drawn image as a guide.

3. Trim the blocks (page 17) to 9¹⁵⁄₁₆″ × 9¹⁵⁄₁₆″ (14⅝″ × 14⅝″). This quilt has a pieced border. In order for the border to fit, the blocks must be trimmed to these exact measurements.

Pieced Blocks

The patterns for the pieced border blocks are on pattern pullout page P4 at the back of the book.

1. Cut 48 quarter-circles and 48 quarter-circle perimeters.

2. Sew each quarter-circle to a perimeter.

Tip

Press the quarter-circle seam allowances toward the perimeter in order to make the perimeter side of the seam slightly higher than the circle side. In this way the pieced circles will be slightly depressed like the background-fabric circles are in the tile blocks.

3. Sew 4 quarter-circle units together to assemble the quarter-circles into 12 blocks.

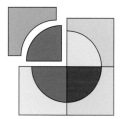

Make 12.

Medallion Corner Triangles

1. Cut 2 squares 15⅛″ × 15⅛″ (22⅛″ × 22⅛″).

2. Cut each square in half diagonally.

3. Sew the corner triangles onto the medallion tile blocks.

Tips

- Some fabrics would be more suitably cut as triangles than half-square triangles. For example, the woven-stripe fabric was cut in triangles with the hypotenuse of the triangle across the width of the fabric in order to radiate the stripes toward the corners. If the fabric you have chosen is of this nature, cut 4 right triangles that measure 15⅛″ (22⅛″) on each side and approximately 21⅜″ (31¼″) on the diagonal.

- If you are using fabric on the bias for the corner triangles, interface the fabric with lightweight fusible interfacing before cutting.

Border

1. Sew 3 pieced circle blocks together in a strip. Make 4.

2. Sew a border corner block to each end of 2 of the strips of pieced blocks.

3. Sew a strip of circle blocks to the top and bottom of the quilt, matching the center seam of the middle circle block with the corner of the medallion.

4. Sew a strip of circle blocks and border corner blocks to each side of the quilt, matching the seams.

Finish the Quilt

1. Layer and baste.

2. Quilt. Shirley Greenhoe designed a beautiful custom quilting pattern using the line drawing of hydrangea blossoms from the printed fabric images and the circle motif. Her quilting highlights those two distinctive elements in a most innovative way—hydrangea blossoms calm the corner triangles as spirals animate the medallion and border.

3. Bind.

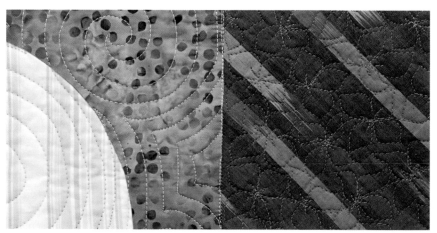

Hydrangea blossoms and spirals in quilting

All in a Dream

All in a Dream, Kathe Dougherty, Lawrence, Kansas;
machine quilted by Lori Kukuk, McLouth, Kansas, 2008

SIZE: 74″ × 74″

BLOCKS: 16″ × 16″ finished

Kathe's quilt is a sophisticated study in warm and cool colors as well as a pleasing balance of stripes with large-scale prints. Each block is made up of three squares, one within another within another. There are cool colors on two sides and warm colors on the other two sides of each block, with crisp divisions between warm and cool thanks to the mitered corners. She arranged the blocks to create an overall pattern of large warm and cool diamonds.

The outer square of each block features large-scale prints; the middle squares are printed stripes, woven stripes, or ikat washes that read as stripes; and the inner square of each block is a print that brings out all the block's colors. Her background fabric and border are a multicolor ikat wash. She carried colors from the tile blocks into the border by machine appliquéing squares on point at the corners of the blocks.

Kathe could have pieced the square-within-a-square-within-a-square blocks, but she avoided the task of piecing 8 mitered corners in each block by using machine appliqué in the tile quilt technique. As a bonus, the resulting grout lines add dramatic diagonal movement to the composition.

The straight-edged pieces of this quilt provide a golden opportunity to learn or practice machine appliqué.

Fabric Requirements

LIGHT IKAT OR PRINT: 5¼ yards for background fabric for tile blocks and border

STRIPES AND LARGE-SCALE PRINTS: ⅛-yard pieces for tile blocks and border diamonds (A large selection—the more the better—will add interest to the quilt. The selection should be divided about equally between warm and cool colors, geometrics and prints. See the note in Tile Blocks, below.)

BACKING: 4⅞ yards

BATTING: 82″ × 82″

BINDING: ⅝ yard for straight-grain double-fold 2″-wide binding

Tile Blocks

The patterns for the tile block are on pattern pullout page P4. Refer to pages 13–15 for needle-turn appliqué, page 16 for machine appliqué, or pages 16–17 for fusible appliqué techniques. However, do not prepare the appliqué pieces as described in those sections. Follow the instructions below to prepare and position the appliqué pieces.

1. Cut 16 squares 18½″ × 18½″ of background fabric.

2. Fold and press each background square diagonally both ways.

3. Make the following freezer-paper or paper-backed fusible adhesive patterns:

- Make 16 using pattern M.
- Make 64 using pattern 1–2–3–4.
- Make 64 using pattern A–B–C–D.

4. Label the following pieces:

- Of the 64 from pattern 1–2–3–4, label 16 with a "1," 16 with a "2", and so on.
- Of the 64 from pattern A–B–C–D, label 16 with an A, 16 with a B, and so on.

5. Audition fabrics and choose 5 for each block.

Note

- A, B, 1, and 2 will be warm colors; C, D, 3, and 4 will be cool colors.

- Within each block, A and B will be the same fabric. Likewise, each of the pairs, C and D, 1 and 2, and 3 and 4, will be the same fabric.

- The fabric chosen for M will reflect all the other colors in the block.

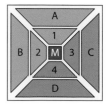

Pattern placement for warm and cool colors

6. For hand or machine appliqué, iron the 9 freezer-paper pattern pieces for a block to the right side of the chosen fabrics, leaving at least ¼" of space around each pattern piece (½" between pieces). For fusible appliqué, iron the paper-backed fusible pattern pieces to the wrong side of the chosen fabrics. No space is needed between the pieces.

7. Cut out the fabric shapes; leave a ¼" seam allowance around the pieces for hand or machine appliqué, or cut on the line for fusible appliqué.

Note

For hand or machine appliqué:

- Press the seam allowances to the wrong side of the fabric. For the trapezoidal pieces, press the diagonal sides first, then the shorter of the parallel sides, and finally the longer parallel side.

- If the 2 sharp points on the trapezoidal pieces seem too bulky, clip approximately half the point away before pressing the seam allowances.

Tip: Use a small dot of basting glue to hold the sharp points together.

8. Peel off the paper from piece M. Place the small fabric square in the center of a square of background fabric, lining it up so that each corner is on a creased diagonal.

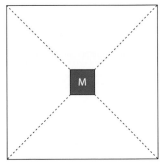

Placement of piece M

9. Pin securely.

10. Appliqué or fuse in place.

11. Peel off the paper from piece 1. Place fabric trapezoid 1 on the background fabric with the short parallel side lined up even with the side of the center

square and leaving ¼" of background fabric (grout) showing between the trapezoid and the square.

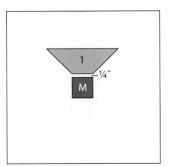

Placement of trapezoid 1

12. Pin securely.

13. Appliqué or fuse in place.

Tip

If you are machine appliquéing and have difficulty appliquéing the sharp points of the trapezoid, stop machine stitching before reaching the points and hand tack them. If you are going to stop stitching before reaching the points, stitch along the shorter parallel side first, turn the corner, and continue down one diagonal side. Then stitch the other diagonal side, and finally stitch the longer parallel side.

14. Peel off the paper from piece 2. Place fabric trapezoid 2 on the background fabric with the short parallel side lined up even with the side of the center square and ¼" of background fabric (grout) showing between trapezoid 2 and the center square and between trapezoids 1 and 2.

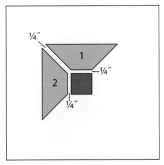

Placement of trapezoid 2

15. Pin securely.

16. Appliqué or fuse in place.

17. Repeat this process for paper patterns 3 and 4.

Note

Kathe emphasized the expanding structure of her block by shortening the outer trapezoidal pieces to increase the width of the diagonal grout between the large trapezoids from ¼″ to approximately ⅝″. For this reason, as you will see in the following instructions, the placement of trapezoids A, B, C, and D differs from that of trapezoids 1, 2, 3, and 4.

18. Peel off the paper from piece A. Place fabric trapezoid A on the background fabric with the short parallel side *lined up even* with the long side of trapezoid 1 and ¼″ of background fabric showing between trapezoids 1 and A.

19. Pin securely.

20. Appliqué or fuse in place.

21. Peel off paper pattern B. Place fabric trapezoid B on the background fabric with the short parallel side *lined up even* with the long side of trapezoid 2 and ¼″ of background fabric showing between trapezoids 2 and B. *There will be approximately ⅝″ of background fabric (grout) showing between trapezoids A and B.*

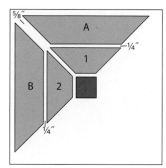

Placement of trapezoids A and B

22. Repeat this process for pieces C and D.

23. Repeat Steps 6–22 for each of the blocks.

24. Trim the blocks (page 17) to 16½″ × 16½″. This quilt has a pieced border. In order for the border to fit, the blocks must be trimmed to these exact measurements.

25. Arrange the blocks in 4 rows to form warm and cool diamonds.

26. Sew the blocks together.

Border

1. Cut 16 squares 4¾″ × 4¾″ of background fabric.

2. Fold and press each square in half lengthwise and crosswise.

3. Prepare 16 M pieces using fabrics left over from the tile blocks.

4. Place a square M on point on a square of background fabric, lining it up so that each corner of M is on a crease.

Placement of piece M for border

5. Pin securely and appliqué or fuse.

6. From background fabric:

- Cut 8 strips 4¾″ × 12½″.
- Cut 8 strips 4¾″ × 14⅝″.

7. Sew 3 squares alternating with 2 strips 4¾″ × 12½″. Make 4.

8. Add a 4¾″ × 14⅝″ strip to each end of each of the 4 units from Step 7.

9. Sew border strips to the top and bottom of the quilt.

10. For the side borders, add a square to each end of the 2 remaining border strips.

11. Sew the side borders to the quilt.

Finish the Quilt

1. Layer and baste.

2. Quilt. The quilting of *All in a Dream* reflects its construction and its fabrics. The outer squares of each block, which are made up of large-scale prints, including many florals, are quilted with curved lines in repeated swirls; the middle squares, which are made up of stripes or fabrics that read as stripes, are quilted with concentric squares. The quilting of the borders mimics the ikat wash fabric with closely stitched lines that swing back and forth.

3. Bind.

Gallery of Contemporary Tile Quilts

Marbled Tiles with Dragonflies, C. Ann Burgess, Leavenworth, Kansas;
machine quilted by Lori Kukuk, McLouth, Kansas, 2008, 60″ × 60″

Ann hand marbled, hand dyed, and hand painted the fabrics in her beautiful tile quilt; the only commercial fabric she used on the top is the batik background fabric in the blocks. Her large, graceful tile shapes show her fabrics to great advantage. Ann's composition is a fascinating mix of dragonfly blocks with some strongly directional geometric blocks and other blocks with an almost tapestry-like overall effect.

Sarah's Quilt, Jackie Turner Greenfield, Lincoln, Nebraska, 2002, 34½″ × 34½″

Jackie made this quilt in memory of her daughter Sarah, whose name appears in the center block. Jackie has volunteered at the International Quilt Study Center since 1997. When she became acquainted with the Hattie Burdick tile quilt (page 7), her brewing interest in reproducing some of the antique quilt patterns coincided perfectly with her desire to use fabric she had saved from Sarah's clothing and accessories. Jackie loved the look produced by the tile quilt technique; she liked being able to use small, significant pieces of fabric without obscuring them in an overall pattern; and she liked having a way to use Sarah's name prominently in her quilt.

A Bird for All Seasons: Summer, Wendy Turnbull, Lawrence, Kansas; machine quilted by Lori Kukuk, McLouth, Kansas, 2008, 40″ × 24″

For her lush depiction of summertime, Wendy drew large, fantastic flowers and leaves, then rendered them in densely patterned prints. She even used patterned fabric for the more typically somber image of the raven, making him fit right into the luxuriant surroundings. Wendy chose a plum color for the background fabric that intensifies the warmth of the tile fabrics. Her first tile quilt has become the first in a series featuring the raven in each season.

Rose Arbor, Ann Rhode, Berkeley, California, 2008, 37″ × 37″

Ann used the traditional tile quilt technique as a means to realize her contemporary creative vision. She combined the tile quilt technique with piecing and regular appliqué, which accommodated her method of working without planning an entire quilt before beginning construction. Using the printed images of roses and rose leaves from Japanese cotton fabric as her point of departure, Ann began with the tile technique and appliquéd the leaves and rose that extend into the border after the center section was complete. She also used several types of quilting, both hand and machine, in finishing her lovely *Rose Arbor*. The hand quilting includes some areas done with heavy thread and large stitches.

Hot Mama, Deb Rowden, Lawrence, Kansas, 2008, 25″ × 28″

Deb made her tile quilt from a drawing done by her 6-year-old daughter, Kate, in 1994. At the time, Kate loved the word "hot" and applied it to everything, even her mama. A child's line drawing makes a perfect tile quilt pattern. And Deb captured the childlike spirit of the original with her cheerfully uninhibited fabric choices.

All in the Family, Bobbi Finley and the Glory Bee, Williamsburg, Virginia, 2008, 36½″ × 36½″

Bobbi designed, assembled, and quilted this feline-festooned nine-patch. Members of a group she regularly sews with, the Glory Bee, helped stitch the blocks. Like some nineteenth-century tile quilt makers, Bobbi used printed fabric images in her quilt. But she departed from the time-honored tile background of random shapes by creating nine different quilt blocks, some more recognizably traditional than others, in which to feature the cats. And she gave *All in the Family* a decidedly contemporary touch by using a plaid background fabric. In the border Bobbi quilted the names of all the cats in her family over the years. A fondness for cats runs in the family!

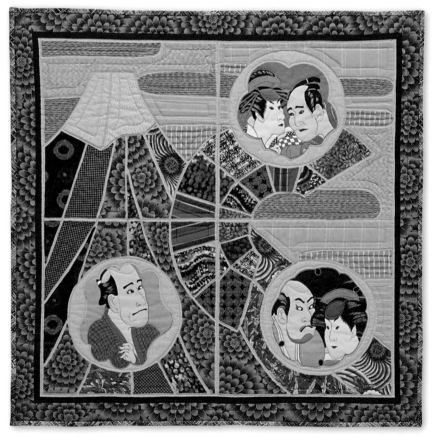

Mt. Fuji Melodrama, Nicki Listerman, Lawrence, Kansas; machine quilted by Lori Kukuk, McLouth, Kansas, 2008, 32½″ × 32½″

This aptly named tableau began with Nicki's interest in using a large-scale print of Kabuki actors in a tile quilt. Nicki teamed up with Carol Gilham Jones, who came up with a drawing, a pastiche of the printed fabric images of the actors together with other familiar Japanese imagery—Mt. Fuji, linear clouds, and a fan. Nicki's fabrics include some Japanese fabrics, in particular, the grayed purples in the mountain, but range widely to achieve the brilliant total effect.

Crayola Magic, Georgann Eglinski, Lawrence, Kansas, 2008, 23¼″ × 17½″

Remember coloring on paper, covering the brilliant colors with black, and then scratching off some of the black to reveal the colors of the rainbow below? That universal childhood activity was the inspiration for Georgann's dazzling quilt. She used a multicolored batik as her background fabric and black fabric for the tile shapes. Georgann completed the theme by machine quilting with rainbow-hued thread and binding with multicolored striped fabric.

Hearts and Flowers for a Friend, Nancy L. Losee, Williamsburg, Virginia, 2008, 24½″ × 24¾″

Nan used elements from a traditional appliqué vocabulary, such as the red hearts surrounding the central star, in creating this charming floral tribute, and she carries the viewer's eye around the central motif with soft sweeping scallops. The high contrast between darks and lights nicely balances the sweetness of the printed fabrics. Likewise, the cool blue background fabric is a foil for the rich, warm red of the hearts and inner border.

Mackintosh Rose, Georgann Eglinski, Lawrence, Kansas, 2008, 14″ × 31¾″

Georgann made this elegant tile quilt from Barbara Brackman's drawing of a rose abstracted in a style popularized by Charles Rennie Mackintosh. In keeping with the refinement of the design, Georgann limited the number of fabrics—there are only two in the lower block—and chose fabrics with very subtle patterning.

Celebration of Collaboration

Reaching for a Star, Bobbi Finley, Williamsburg, Virginia, and Carol Gilham Jones, Lawrence, Kansas, 2008, 22¾" × 24"

> We love working together on quilts, and we encourage you to have a go at collaboration. A tile quilt is an ideal project to share with a friend or friends.

We have found that even the distance between our homes in Virginia and Kansas is not much of an obstacle to collaborating. With *Starry Orange Peel* (page 27), we planned the quilt together and divided the labor of executing it. We began by looking at historical tile quilts and found one we were particularly inspired by that had design elements we thought would work well for our first attempt to design our own tile quilt. By telephone and in email conversations, we decided on the number and size of tile blocks and the palette and fabrics for the tile pieces, and, finally together in a quilt shop, on a background fabric. Sitting next to each other at a quilt retreat, we designed and began stitching the first two blocks. After returning home, we stitched independently until all nine of the tile blocks were done. After auditioning various block arrangements and border fabrics, and emailing photos to Carol for her suggestions, Bobbi sewed the top together and quilted the blocks; Carol quilted the borders and added the binding. Needless to say, the USPS and the Internet were indispensable partners in this collaboration.

Email was our silent partner for *Reaching for a Star* (above). Through exchanged messages we agreed on the theme, size, and fabric; Carol made a drawing, scanned it, and sent it to Bobbi. In order to agree on the fabric layout, we again used the scanner and electronic messaging. With all the decisions made, Carol began the stitching and turned it over to Bobbi when we rendezvoused for a weekend.

As a quilter, you can spend an awful lot of time working by yourself. For certain projects, isolation may be desirable or even necessary. But for the most part, quilting projects benefit from shared ideas, compounded creativity, and extra energy. And the collaborating quilters relish their collective experience. We encourage you to find a friend and start your own collaboration.

About the Authors

Photo courtesy of Deb Rowden

Carol Gilham Jones and Bobbi Finley

Carol Gilham Jones lives in Lawrence, Kansas, with her sweetheart, Charles, and their dogs, Sumo and Grace. Bobbi Finley now resides back in her native state in San Jose, California, with her cat, Thomas, after residing for a while in Williamsburg, Virginia. Bobbi and Carol had the great good fortune to meet at a San Francisco Bay Area quilting retreat in 1990. The friendship that grew out of that meeting soon included working together on quilts. Their first collaboration, documented in "We Came, We Sewed, We Conquered," *American Quilter* Vol. XV, No. 3, has been followed by many others. In 2006, with both at last retired, they got around to making their first tile quilt, a long-contemplated project.

Bobbi makes prize-winning quilts, has a quilt in the collection of the American Museum of Folk Art in New York, and has exhibited at the International Quilt Festival in Houston and American Quilter's Society in Paducah, Kentucky. Her love for exploring the history of quilts and their makers has led her to actively participate in the American Quilt Study Group, serving as a board member and co-curator of the study quilt exhibits.

Carol's quilts have twice appeared on the cover of the magazine *Quilters Newsletter,* and her quilts have been included in a show at the Autry Museum of Western Heritage in Los Angeles. In 2004 and 2005, a quilt she made with Bobbi and Georgann Eglinski traveled around Japan in *Japanese Imagery in One Hundred Quilts.*

Great Titles *from* C&T PUBLISHING

Available at your local retailer or **www.ctpub.com** *or* **800-284-1114**

For a list of other fine books from C&T Publishing,
visit our website to view our catalog online:

C&T PUBLISHING, INC.

P.O. Box 1456
Lafayette, CA 94549
800-284-1114

Email: ctinfo@ctpub.com
Website: www.ctpub.com

Tips and Techniques can be found at www.ctpub.com > Consumer
Resources > Quiltmaking Basics: Tips & Techniques for Quiltmaking & More

C&T Publishing's professional photography services are now available to
the public. Visit us at www.ctmediaservices.com.

For quilting supplies:

COTTON PATCH

1025 Brown Ave.
Lafayette, CA 94549
Store: 925-284-1177
Mail order: 925-283-7883

Email: CottonPa@aol.com
Website: www.quiltusa.com

Note: Fabrics used in the quilts shown may not be currently
available, as fabric manufacturers keep most fabrics in print for
only a short time.